presented to

Pat & Gene

by

Brenda & Bill

on this date

May 31, 1999

Thank You

RAY BOLTZ

Moments

of Gratitude

from the Heart

Foreword

"Sure!"

That's what I said when Georgia Richardson asked me to write a special song for "Pastor Appreciation Day." I had about eight weeks to write the song and figured that would be plenty of time. After all there were so many things I could say about our pastor, Eldon Morehouse.

I have heard a lot of great preachers and teachers in my time, but Eldon Morehouse is more than a preacher—he's a *pastor*. There's a difference. Preachers use their words to make an impact. Eldon uses his life.

When Eldon speaks, you never get the feeling he is trying to build a kingdom for himself. Instead, you feel he is more interested in you than his position. More interested in God using you than God using him. But how do you express those kinds of things in song? Eight weeks flew by.

The night before "Pastor Appreciation Day" I was sitting alone at my old piano trying to write that song, but the words just wouldn't come. How could I convey how much Eldon's encouragement had meant through the years, without sounding silly?

I began to think of others who had made an impact on my life, and I could see some common threads. First, many of those people were in heaven. I remembered Rev. Harry Jones, who came to the tiny Methodist church my parents attended when I was a child. He was a retired minister, but was willing to take the church when no one else would. He also took the time to sit down with a twelve-year-old boy and lead him to Jesus.

*S*econd, these people were not famous. Most of them had never received honor or applause for their efforts. They had never received a medal or had a curtain call. They were Sunday school teachers, neighbors, parents, relatives, scout leaders, coaches—people who had deeply affected my life but had never received thanks for their efforts.

*R*eminiscing about these unsung heroes got me to thinking that maybe the best way for me to honor Eldon was to honor all those caring individuals who give and give without recognition and applause. It also made me realize that no matter how much appreciation we try to show others, we can never match the appreciation that will be showered on them when they walk into heaven. That is where the real rewards will be handed out.

*T*he song began . . . and so did the journey.

"I dreamed I went to heaven and you were there with me . . ."

RAY BOLTZ

Thank You

LYRICS AND MUSIC BY RAY BOLTZ

I dreamed I went to heaven
And you were there with me
We walked upon the streets of gold
Beside the crystal sea
We heard the angels singing
Then someone called your name
You turned and saw this young man
And he was smiling as he came

And he said friend you may not know me now
And then he said but wait
You used to teach my Sunday school
When I was only eight
And every week you would say a prayer
Before the class would start
And one day when you said that prayer
I asked Jesus in my heart

CHORUS:
Thank you for giving to the Lord
I am a life that was changed
Thank you for giving to the Lord
I am so glad you gave

Then another man stood before you
And said remember the time
A missionary came to your church
And his pictures made you cry
You didn't have much money
But you gave it anyway
Jesus took the gift you gave
And that's why I am here today

[REPEAT CHORUS]
One by one they came
Far as the eye could see
Each life somehow touched
By your generosity
Little things that you had done
Sacrifices made
Unnoticed on the earth
In heaven now proclaimed

And I know up in heaven
You're not supposed to cry
But I am almost sure
There were tears in your eyes
As Jesus took your hand
And you stood before the Lord
He said my child look around you
Great is your reward

[REPEAT CHORUS TWICE]
I am so glad you gave

The Bicycle Man

Sometimes there are people you never have the chance to thank, people who never knew how much they helped you. For me, this person was a bicycle man.

I was eighteen and alone on a bicycle trip through France, trying to survive on ten dollars a day. Halfway up a mountain in central France the crankshaft of my bicycle seized up. The pedals were almost impossible to turn.

It was an isolated road. I was hungry and broke and across the ocean from home in a country where I hardly understood the language. I didn't even have the option of quitting.

Two discouraging and exhausting hours later, I finally reached a small town. I found a bicycle shop, cluttered with old-fashioned bikes. A tiny old man, wearing a greasy apron, graciously ignored my horrible attempts at French. He wordlessly assessed the condition of my bicycle, fixed it, and waved away the money I offered to him. With a sudden big grin, he gave me a thumbs up and sent me on my way.

Looking back, I suspect he understood better than I how much I needed his help. Often, these small kindnesses reflect Christ's love far more than grand gestures. To the bicycle man I want to say, "Thanks!"

SIGMUND BROUWER

Thank You

RAY BOLTZ

Dear Mother and Daddy,

Thank you for knowing when to say "no" despite my childish anger and when to say "yes" despite my teenage reluctance.

Thank you for the lessons of hard work, honesty, friendship, forgiveness, community, courage, conviction, and contribution.

Thank you for loving me, my spouse, my children, and my friends.

Thank you for staying just close enough to hear me call when I needed you and far enough away to let me try my wings.

Thank you for asking about my day, my job, and my life—and for not offering unsolicited advice, pronouncements, guilt, or obligations.

Thank you for always being there through sickness, disappointments, confusions, and dreams.

Thank you for modeling commitment, service, and gratitude in your walk with the Lord.

Thank you for the memories of childhood, the guidance of my teen years, the freedom of adulthood, a model for grandparenting, the grace of God, and serenity in aging.

All my love,
DIANNA BOOHER

Thank You, Grandma Graber

I want to tell you about someone who is very special to me. That person is my Grandma Graber, who died on Thanksgiving day in 1988. She was eighty-five years old. In the eight months between the day she had a stroke and the day she breathed her last, I learned as much about being a Christian as I ever have.

*G*randma kept apologizing to us for being a burden, even though we considered it an honor to go to the nursing home to help take care of her. She was a proud woman. To her, being taken care of like a baby was humiliating. Every time the nurses moved her she would scream out in pain. Her skinny little arms were bruised from all the shots and IV's. But she never once complained. In fact, she kept telling us how good Jesus had been to her. And the last thing she did before slipping into a final coma was to hold a picture of Jesus to her cheek and kiss it.

*M*y grandma wasn't rich, and she never finished grade school, but I won't ever be able to find enough words to say what I think about her. And if I could have her back just long enough to say one thing, it would be "Thank you, Grandma, thank you."

SUSAN L. RISNER

Thank you, God:

*F*or my parents, who taught us seven kids respect for authority and taught us that even though we were poor in material things, we were rich in spiritual things.

*F*or healing me of rickets when I was four years old and given six months to live.

*F*or my guardian angel.

*F*or my beautiful wife, Iwalani, and my healthy daughter, Donnette.

*F*or revealing to me that I was to do the work of Jesus, giving to others yet never expecting to get anything back.

*F*or allowing me to provide two schools where disadvantaged children can go to get another chance in life. This enables them to grow and to learn how to give something good back to others.

*F*or the opportunity to play golf for a living and to participate in tournaments like the Legends of Golf for Seniors.

*T*hat I am at peace with myself and am prepared to accept Your perfect will for my life.

CHICHI RODRIGUEZ

I dreamed I went to heaven
And you were there with me

We walked upon the streets of gold
Beside the crystal sea

We heard the angels singing
Then someone called your name

You turned and saw this young man
And he was smiling as he came

Thank You
RAY BOLTZ

Dear Valerie,

I will never forget the day we met. We were both interviewing for positions in the same company. You had a sweet smile and a confident demeanor, and I was divided in my opinion of you. *That girl has it all together!* and *I'm out of a job if I'm competing with her!* ran through my mind simultaneously. A few weeks later, we were on a plane headed for Dallas to train for our new jobs—me, a plain country girl from Kentucky, and you, a bright and talented woman with everything under control. We had both made it!

*O*nly a few months have passed since that day and yet, you have quickly become one of the most important people in my life. You have endured my endless lamentations on every topic, ranging from the slightly ridiculous to the totally absurd. You have shared my sorrows and my joys. You have made me laugh. But most importantly, you have challenged me to become a better person for Christ.

*T*hank you for being my best friend.

Missy
MELISSA PAYNE

Loved and Comforted

*W*hen I was growing up, my father was a Volkswagen mechanic and my mother worked odd jobs trying to support a family of six. As soon as my dad walked in the door we all pounced on him, so glad for him to be home.

*T*hen we turned the TV on and watched our favorite show, *Andy Griffith*. It was such a simple thing but it has made a lifelong impression on me. As I travel around to concerts there are days when I feel weary and homesick. Sometimes I search the TV stations to find an episode of the *Andy Griffith* show, and suddenly I am carried back to my father's lap and the feeling of being loved and comforted—and at home.

*M*y mother was always the strong spiritual influence in our family. She was constantly reading the Bible aloud to us, filling our heads with Scripture. Even though there were times when we simply didn't want to listen, it stuck with us.

I will never be able to thank my parents enough for raising me in a home filled with love, discipline, and Christian beliefs. It has helped me in everything I have been through in my life. They sacrificed their own dreams and desires to give us a warm and loving home. I pray one day that my husband and I can do that same for our children.

CINDY MORGAN

Thank You
RAY BOLTZ

Dear Mrs. Wright,

I came into your seventh-grade geography class with an enormous inferiority complex. I had nurtured it for three years. Since failing third grade, I had been at odds with the school system and with myself. Mentally, I had labeled myself a "loser" and was doing a good job of living up to it.

*T*hat's why I was so surprised to read your affirming notes on my papers. You took the time to praise even the smallest effort. And I still remember so clearly the day you asked me to stay after school for a conference. That thirty-minute visit changed my life.

*Y*ou told me you believed in me and thought I had great academic potential. I was amazed! Your confidence in me boosted my self-esteem and lifted me out of a "loser" mentality. In fact, it boosted me high enough to carry me through fourteen more years of schooling to earn two master's degrees and a doctorate with honors.

*T*he confidence you showed in me has also impacted how I interact with my students. I regularly take time to visit individually with them, encouraging them and reminding them of their potential. I want to repeat the miracle you gave to me.

*T*hank you Mrs. Wright for thirty minutes that changed my life.

DR. CARL BOYD GIBBS

Thank You

RAY BOLTZ

God has woven many wonderful friendships through the tapestry of my life but there are two threads that are outstanding among them all, my husband and my daughter. . . my two best friends.

Dear Michelle

*I*t is my privilege to be your mother, to watch you grow into the godly young woman, wife, and mother that you are. I love just being with you . . . laughing, dreaming, sharing hopes and fears, and encouraging one another. Thank you for being you.

Love,
MOM

Dear Michael,

*I*t is my privilege to be your wife, to know you and to love you. You are to me the greatest example of God's unconditional love—always faithful and enduring so much. You listen when I just need to talk. You encourage me when I want to give up. You hold me when I just need to cry. You believe in me when I see no reason why. Thank you for being the husband you are.

Love,
KARLA DORNACHER

Friend

And he said friend you may not know me now

And then he said but wait

You used to teach my Sunday school

When I was only eight,

And every week you would say a prayer
Before the class would start

And one day when you said that prayer
I asked Jesus in my heart

Thank You

RAY BOLTZ

A Package of Lovingkindness

The happy disposition and quick, easy laughter of my older (and thinner) sister has made me so thankful for her... the laughter is so spontaneous and sort of bubbles out of her with ease.

When we would visit her in Minnesota, she would get up early the morning we were to drive back to California and the smell of chocolate cookies and brownies wafted through the house as she packed a huge lunch for us to take on the trip. So we would be carrying this large package of lovingkindness from her—which usually lasted until we got to South Dakota.

Many years ago I was visiting her and wanted to dye a bathing suit black. I did this dastardly deed and the garment came out a lovely jet black... however, the inside of the washing machine was also jet black—even the rubber ring at the top and the entire tub inside. I was mortified at what I had done, but she just laughed and said she would dump some Clorox into it and all would be fine. And she did... and it was.

It is that immediate response she has of making light out of something that is really dark that makes me so thankful for my sister, Janet.

BARBARA JOHNSON

Thank You, Tim

You taught us to love unconditionally, to look, yearn, and pray from the viewpoint of the prodigal's Father.

You showed us intimate fellowship with the Lord in intense suffering.

You encouraged us with your worship and praise in the deep dungeon of hopelessness.

You taught us to treasure each hour, without borrowing from tomorrow.

You gave a reality to all we had known about dying and presented eternity with a sweeter meaning to us.

Your mother and I never dreamed that you would embrace Heaven at thirty years of age, on your birthday.

The experience we shared with you, when you went into "a far country," contracted AIDS, and returned to repentance and deliverance was something we thought happened to others—surely not to our family.

God was so good to allow us to walk with you through your darkest valley. We will love you always.

MALCOLM AND JOHNIE GRAINGER

Dear Kathy,

You mean everything to me. I'm excited about our future, and I'm so grateful I get to spend it with you. It would be infinitely more sobering, less secure, more boring, and less lovely without you.

You never finish finding ways of showing your love. I pray I can do the same. You fill up my life. I love you—forever.

I am convinced that nothing in all creation, neither heights nor depths, things above nor things below, principalities nor powers, life nor death, can separate you from my life and love.

Through the times of trial, pain, and heartache, and through the times of pride, gratitude, and joy, there is no other with whom I can imagine sharing these times more intimately and meaningfully. My mind cannot find words adequate to express the depth of my love for you. My love for you is beyond telling: It is a major part of all that is me.

I hope this year is very special for you, and that I can play a part in making it special.

Your loving husband,
KIP JORDON

Thank You, Kip

My husband, Kip Jordan, entered Baylor Hospital on October 27, 1997. He had slipped into a coma caused by too much ammonia in his body—the result of a diseased liver. The ammonia levels were going down, and I assumed he would be fine again, as always. But, on October 30, the ammonia level was so high he could not come back to us.

We had not said "good-bye." I had not said, "Thank you, Kip." I would like to thank him now:

Thank you, my darling Kip, for the privilege of sharing your life as your wife for thirty-two years.

Thank you for tag-parenting our sons—when I could not cope, I said, "Tag, you're it. . ." and you became the primary parent. Thank you for loving our boys so intensely.

Thank you for reading the same books I read and discussing them with me so we could grow together.

Thank you for sharing with me your love of all people, of books, of authors, of ideas, of dreams and visions, of Scripture, of the church.

Thank you for your gift to touch and for holding me in your arms as we slept.

Thank you for being so fun and for teasing me out of my seriousness.

Thank you for being the man my mother could love as her own son.

Thank you for seeing the good, despite the flaws, of your family, friends, co-workers, and authors.

Thank you for following Christ. I know where you are now and Whom you are with.

Your loving wife,
KATHY JORDAN

Giving

Thank you for giving to the Lord

I am a life that was changed

Thank you for giving to the Lord

I am so glad you gave

Then another man stood before you
And said remember the time

A missionary came to your church
And his pictures made you cry

Thank You Mom and Dad

I would like to thank my parents for their unwavering commitment to Christ through thick and thin and for the example they have led my entire life. I would especially like to thank them for dedicating my life to the Lord as a child—committing their child to the will of the Lord, not expecting anything more than for His perfect will to be laid out as the path that would lead me through life.

I am so thankful my parents never forced me into a career, only encouraged me to do what God called me to do and to do it to the best of my ability.

I am so thankful my parents have always supported and encouraged me. Had they imposed their personal will on my life, I would have missed out on the greatest privilege and adventure—traveling around the world as a missionary photographer, sharing through images what the Lord is doing through missions.

DAVID DOBSON

I Will Never Forget Mr. Langley

My last year at Christ the King Elementary School, I had the best teacher and friend one could ever come across. His name is Larry L. Langley, and I want to take this time to let him know how much I appreciated his happy smile every morning and afternoon.

There are so many memories a girl can have from grade school, but those with Mr. Langley were the best. He always had a story to tell. I will never forget seeing *Phantom of the Opera* in New York on our class trip, talking with him almost every morning at seven or earlier.

I am most thankful to him for being my confirmation sponsor. I will never forget the lessons I learned that year, and I know I will never forget Mr. Langley. People these days do not know where all the good people have gone. If they really want to meet one, they should meet Mr. Larry Langley.

ROSEANNE M. YORK
(15 years old)

Thank You

RAY BOLTZ

Thank You
RAY BOLTZ

Cris, my love, my heart,

As an instrument of God, you saved my life. Thank you for giving me another chance to be your husband, to share our children's lives and our walk with the Lord. Thank you for giving me and the kids so much—no book would have enough room to hold my thanks for who you are and what you mean to me.

NICK

Nick, my husband, my love,

Thank you for opening your heart to the Lord and to me.
I feel your love, your tender touch and your forgiveness. You teach, guide, and help me grow. I thank you for accepting His leadership for our family, and for allowing me another chance to be your wife and to make memories with our children as we build our future together.

CRIS

We were married for 9 years.
We were divorced nearly 3 years.
We remarried April, 1998.
We have been given a second chance.
To God be the Glory!

NICK AND CRIS PALAFOX

Thank You, Chuck Swindoll!

*I*n 1978, I was a young seminary student whose beliefs began to be questioned by liberal theology. One morning, driving to campus, I heard a radio broadcast—Charles [Chuck] Swindoll was teaching from the book of James. I was impressed with his razor-sharp mind and passionate heart. He had the balance I wanted in life and in ministry. I made a decision right then to have a mind committed to the Lordship of Christ and a heart that burned with passion for Him and His Word.

*T*wenty years later, I became the Chairman of the Board of Trustees at the seminary I had attended. On the day we installed a new president, whose dynamic leadership would bring a renewed faithfulness to God's Word, I couldn't help but think of the thanks I owed this man:

*T*hanks, Chuck , for your dedication to Scripture. You have influenced my life and the lives of thousands who will pass through the halls of this seminary in years to come.

"The things which you have heard from Me . . . these entrust to faithful men, who will be able to teach others also" (2 Timothy 2:2).

RICK WHITE

You didn't have much money

But you gave it anyway

Jesus took the gift you gave
And that's why I am here today

One by one they came
Far as the eye could see

Each life somehow touched
By your generosity

Little things that you had done
Sacrifices made
Unnoticed on the earth
In heaven now proclaimed

Thank You.

RAY BOLTZ

God's Gift to Me

My wife is my greatest gift from God. I was initially attracted to her because she was beautiful. She also had a sweet Christian spirit with a lovely temperament. By contrast, I've always been a tornado, a fast-lane fireball.

Four months after we met, I asked her to marry me. I felt she would make a great wife. That was the best decision I ever made. I knew she would be perfect for me as I anticipated the pressure I would face in the business world.

Thanks, Peggy, for giving me the opportunity to be your husband. You are not only a lover of God, but a lover of me. You are honest, steady, easygoing, and persistent in staying by my side all these years.

I thank God for your compassion, hospitality, love, and warmth. You have faithfully encouraged me at every turn.

Thank you, Peggy. I love you.
SAM MOORE

Carolyn,

*T*he two words *thank you* are simply not enough. You are the most caring, gentle, and accepting person I know. You never fail to honor the court jester in me—that fanciful writer's spirit that so often drives you mad. For your acceptance of all that I am, I thank you. With you there are no meaningless moments: whether it's enjoying a *latte* together on an impromptu date in the afternoon, or holding hands as we stroll Balboa Island—saying nothing, and in the depth of our stillness, saying everything. For always being there, I can only say "thank you."

*E*verything about you inspires me. Your tender heart toward those who suffer touches me. From the break of day until the blazing sun falls quietly beneath the horizon, you are both the giving and the gift. For who you are, and what you are helping me to become, I thank you. Today. Tomorrow. Forever.

ROBERT C. LARSON

Thank You, Grandpa Dourte

One of my earliest recollections of Grandpa Dourte is standing in his workshop as a nine-year-old boy, warming my backside at the little cast iron stove in the corner. In the dead of winter, while his fields slept, my granddaddy built things. I marveled at his meticulous craftsmanship, even though he had lost all the fingers of his left hand forty years before. I treasured time with him because of his quick wit and light heart. Most of all, I admired his unwavering love for God. The perpetual humming of old hymns, his spontaneous recalling of many Psalms and poems by memory, and the twinkle in his eye gave this impressionable youngster the idea that hard work, painstaking attention to detail, and a commitment to the Heavenly Father were the marks of a truly great man.

Years later at Grandpa's memorial service, one of his sons read his will: "I leave to my family something that does not have to be divided among them . . . something that can be received by each one in full measure. I leave to my eight children, thirty-five grandchildren, eighty-six great grandchildren, and twelve great, great, grandchildren, my love for my Heavenly Father."

Monroe Dourte left his family a legacy of faith—countless hours of prayer on his knees, immense portions of memorized Scripture, a love for hymns, and a heart for God. As a member of this fortunate clan, I inherited this patriarchal grant in total.

Thank you, Grandpa Dourte. Thank you for your hard work. Thank you for your attention to detail. Thank you for your good humor and tender smile. And thank you for my inheritance. I will be eternally grateful.

ROBERT WOLGEMUTH

And I know up in heaven
You're not supposed to cry

But I am almost sure
There were tears in your eyes

As Jesus took your hand
And you stood before the Lord

He said my child look around you
Great is your reward

I am so glad you gave

Dear Mom and Dad,

*W*hat an incredible legacy you have given us! Through fifty years of marriage, you have shown us your faithfulness. You always treated each other with love and respect, never calling attention to each other's faults and shortcomings. You taught us how to serve, how to put others first and how to love. By your example, we learned how to treat others, especially our spouses. We know that, daily, you bring our families and each one of us by name before the throne of God in prayer. All our lives continue to be touched by this special gift. Thank you both for letting God demonstrate His faithfulness through your lives. We are grateful for the support you have given and for the example you continue to be to each of us. We feel truly blessed to be your children. We love you and pray you will have many more years together to serve our Lord.

We love you!
STEVE, EL, LEE, AND NATE

Thank You

RAY BOLTZ

A Gentle Servant's Heart

*F*rom the first time we met twenty-five years ago, I knew there was something special about him—a kindness, a gentleness. Today I know it is a servant's heart of compassion.

*O*ur first years together flew by. We married young and soon had two boys to raise. As life progressed and we prospered, times got tough. We suffered a huge financial loss with a business and personal bankruptcy. The silver lining seemed to have fallen out of the black cloud that clung to us. In those worst of times, as in the best, he continued to seek God's counsel and direction for his family, and to sacrifice himself for others.

*T*hough his wall has few trophies, I have seen the numerous stranded motorists he has rescued, the ex-convicts he has given a new start, and the poor and desperate for whom he has fought for justice. As a faithful father and husband, he goes without to give to his family and others. He encourages, supports, rescues, loves, and forgives. He is a man of compassion, a true servant of God.

Thank you Doug, for giving to the Lord—and to me. I love you.
DEBBIE WICKWIRE

Thank You

RAY BOLTZ

Dear Mr. Boltz,

I work as a nurse in a nursing home and chronic health hospital. Several months ago Mrs. Brokaw came to live here. She is an eighty-five-year-old widow with no children. She has a master's degree in foreign languages and taught German, Spanish, French, and Latin in the high school I attended. Mrs. Brokaw is also a very sincere and dedicated Christian. She taught Sunday school for over fifty years until she was physically incapable of doing it any longer. She was my Sunday school teacher for two years when I was nine and ten years old.

*B*ecause I was working the night shift, I only saw Mrs. Brokaw briefly two or three times a month. But several weeks ago I was offered a position as nurse on an earlier shift. About that time a local radio station frequently played your song "Thank You." Whenever I heard that song I would think of Mrs. Brokaw and what she had done for so many kids through the years.

*O*ne day I decided to write her a letter explaining about the song, and I wrote the lyrics out for her. In the letter I thanked her for the positive influence she had had on my life and on the lives of so many other young people. I told her I was sure that when she went to heaven, God would have a great reward waiting for her.

*I*n the course of my duties I passed her door three times in a half hour after handing her the letter, and each time she was holding it and reading it over and over. Later when I went to her room she hugged me and told me she was thrilled. Since then we have grown very close. I spend a minute or two with her as often as I can. We talk and then I kiss her and tell her I love her.

I am ashamed to admit that without the nudging your song gave me, I might never have had the thoughtfulness to express my thanks to Mrs. Brokaw—and we would both have been the poorer for it.

Thank you Mr. Boltz.
Leila Cook

Thank You

RAY BOLTZ

Facing the Bunkers

I am thankful for the adversity, the "bunkers of life," that God has placed in my path to refine my character and give me opportunity to fulfill His purpose. Suffering with severe clinical depression in recent years led to the loss of my career as a corporate executive—and near suicide. But God used these circumstances to fulfill my heart's desire to write and speak to golfers about life and faith.

*G*od led me to the best book designers and publishers to provide a platform to communicate the parallels between golf and a life of faith. He provided co-authors who share my passion and people to encourage me to keep going. I am thankful to those people and ultimately to God who promised that "The steps of a man are from the Lord, . . . though he fall, he shall not be cast headlong, for the Lord is the stay of his hand" (Psalm 37:23–24).

*I*n difficult times, it is hard to "count it all joy" and to realize that "the testing of your faith produces steadfastness." I am thankful my character is being refined by these "bunkers" so that, in Him, I will become "complete, lacking in nothing" (James 1:2–4).

JIM SHEARD, PH.D.

From the Publisher

The two words *thank you* could be considered some of the most important words we may ever speak. They will give a person comfort, build confidence, and contribute to their self-esteem. Words of appreciation are so often neglected and *thank you* is a genuine display of that attribute.

I am so thankful for my lovely wife, Marsha, who through the years has been my best friend, greatest cheerleader, wise counselor and someone who has never failed me in any circumstance. She always makes me feel as if I can climb the highest mountain and achieve whatever task I have chosen.

It is my prayer that through this book, you may be encouraged to say "thank you" to someone who has touched your life.

Let me say "thank you" to all of those who played a part in making this book a reality.

JACK COUNTRYMAN
Touching Lives…Changing Lives